Emma,
I couldn't find
Barleysugar, hope
this is a suitable
substitute!
love Joy x x
x

MY CAT JEOFFRY

PELHAM BOOKS

Published by the Penguin Group 27 Wrights Lane, London W8 5TZ, England
Viking Penguin Inc., 375 Hudson Street, New York, New York 10014, USA
Penguin Books Australia Ltd, Ringwood, Victoria, Australia
Penguin Books Canada Ltd, 10 Alcorn Avenue, Toronto, Ontario, Canada M4V 3B2
Penguin Books (NZ) Ltd, 182-190 Wairau Road, Auckland 10, New Zealand

Penguin Books Ltd, Registered Offices: Harmondsworth, Middlesex, England

First published 1992

Copyright © Jill and Martin Leman 1992

Made and printed in
Great Britain by William Clowes Limited,
Beccles and London.

Typeset by Panache, London

A CIP catalogue record for this book is available from the British Library

ISBN 0 7207 2018 4

Martin Leman

MY CAT
JEOFFRY

A POEM BY
CHRISTOPHER SMART

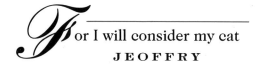

For I will consider my cat
JEOFFRY

For he is the servant of the Living
God, duly and daily serving him.

For at the first glance of the glory
of God in the East he worships
in his way.

For this is done by wreathing his
body seven times round with
elegant quickness.

*F*or then he leaps up to catch the musk, which is the blessing of God upon his prayer.

For he rolls upon prank to work it in.

For having done duty and received blessing he begins to consider himself.

For this he performs in ten degrees.

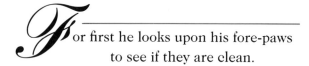

For first he looks upon his fore-paws
to see if they are clean.

For secondly he kicks up behind
to clear away there.

For thirdly he works it upon stretch
with the fore-paws extended.

For fourthly he sharpens
his paws by wood.

For fifthly he washes himself.

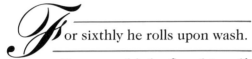

For sixthly he rolls upon wash.

For seventhly he fleas himself,
that he may not be interrupted upon
the beat.

For eighthly he rubs himself
against a post.

For ninthly he looks up for his
instructions.

For tenthly he goes in quest of food.

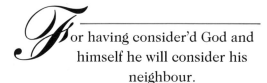

or having consider'd God and himself he will consider his neighbour.

For if he meets another cat he will kiss her in kindness.

For when he takes his prey he plays with it to give it a chance.

For one mouse in seven escapes by his dallying.

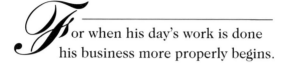

*F*or when his day's work is done his business more properly begins.

For he keeps the Lord's watch in the night against the adversary.

For he counteracts the powers of darkness by his electrical skin and glaring eyes.

For he counteracts the Devil, who is death, by brisking about the life.

*F*or in his morning orisons he loves
the sun and the sun loves him.

For he is of the tribe of Tiger.

For the Cherub Cat is a term of
the Angel Tiger.

For he has the subtlety and hissing
of a serpent, which in goodness
he suppresses.

*F*or he will not do destruction,
if he is well-fed, neither will he
spit without provocation.

For he purrs in thankfulness,
when God tells him he's a good Cat.

For he is an instrument for the
children to learn benevolence upon.

For every house is incomplete without
him and a blessing is lacking
in the spirit.

*F*or the Lord commanded Moses concerning the cats at the departure of the Children of Israel from Egypt.

For every family had one cat at least in the bag.

For the English Cats are the best in Europe.

For he is the cleanest in the use of his fore-paws of any quadrupede.

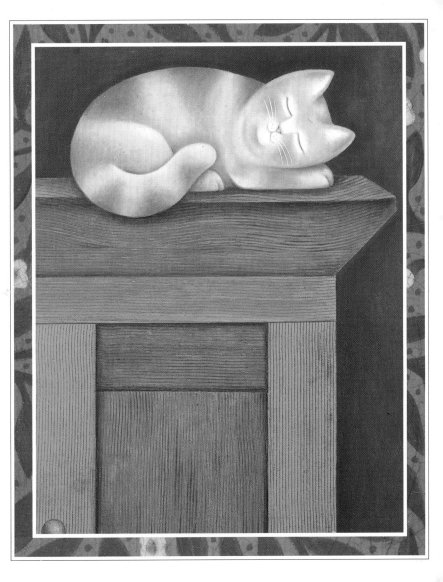

*F*or his tongue is exceeding pure
so that it has in purity what it wants
in musick.

For he is docile and can learn
certain things.

For he can set up with gravity which
is patience upon approbation.

For he can fetch and carry, which is
patience in employment.

For he can jump over a stick
which is patience upon proof positive.

For he can spraggle upon waggle
at the word of command.

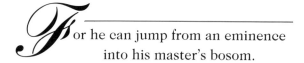

For he can jump from an eminence
into his master's bosom.

For he can catch the cork and
toss it again.

For he is hated by the hypocrite and
miser.

For the former is afraid of detection.

For the latter refuses the charge.

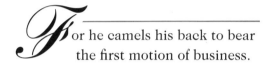

or he camels his back to bear
the first motion of business.

For he is good to think on, if a man
would express himself neatly.

For he made a great figure in Egypt
for his signal services.

For he killed the Ichneumon-rat very
pernicious by land.

*F*or his ears are so acute that they
sting again.

For from this proceeds the passing
quickness of his attention.

For by stroking of him I have found
out electricity.

For I perceived God's light about him
both wax and fire.

For the Electrical fire is the spiritual
substance, which God sends from heaven to
sustain the bodies both of man and beast.

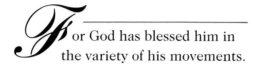

or God has blessed him in
the variety of his movements.

For, tho' he cannot fly, he is an
excellent clamberer.

For his motions upon the face of the
earth are more than any other quadrupede.

For he can tread to all the measures
upon the musick.

For he can swim for life.

For he can creep.